# All Rise:
# Order In The Church
A Practical Guide for Church Etiquette &
Church Behavior

Rogers W. Jackson

Hi Dad,
I thought you might
like to Read this book.
Hope it's useful.
Love
Mom

The Pearls of Great Price Ministries books and motivational tapes may be purchased for motivational, inspirational or sales promotional use. For information please write: Sales Manager, The Pearls of Great Price Ministries, Inc., P.O. Box 362146 Decatur, Georgia 30036.

SECOND EDITION
ISBN # 0-9744057-0-1

Cover Design by:
AWP Designs
Daniel Perry

Layout Design by:
CRoss Media, Graphics & Design
Atlanta, Georgia
Email: crossMGD@bellsouth.net

Printing by:
Atlanta: Sturdivant and Son Printing
268 Edgewood
Atlanta, GA 30303

## Books by Dr. William E. Flippin, Sr.

*Church Etiquette & Church Behavior*
*A Practical guide for Church Behavior in the Black Church*

*A Handbook for Associate Ministers*

*Workbook for Black Churches*
*Reaching College Students*

## The Pearls of Great Price Ministries
## NEW RELEASES

A three part series:

*ALL RISE: Order in the Pulpit*
*A Practical Guide for Associate Ministers*
By Dr. William E. Flippin, Sr.
(August 2003)

*ALL RISE: Order in the Ministry*
*A Practical Guide for Church Administration*
By James McWhorter
(December 2003)

*IN MY FATHER'S HOUSE*
*A Collection of Spiritual Sermons*
By Dr. William E. Flippin, Sr., the Flippin Sons Trio
& Associate Ministers
(August 2003)

# Contents

# CHAPTER 2

## The Charges and The Claims

Twelve Summary Points:

| | |
|---|---|
| One | Be on time. |
| Two | Never pass up the aisle during prayer or scripture reading. |
| Three | Be respectful of the worship service. |
| Four | Be devout in every attitude. |
| Five | Be thoughtful of the comfort of others. |
| Six | Speak a bright cheery word to as many as possible. |
| Seven | Proper address the pulpit and church body. |
| Eight | Never put on your coat or wrap during the closing hymn. |
| Nine | There should be no loud talking or jesting after the service is concluded. |
| Ten | Let reverence be the keyword. |
| Eleven | During prayer, all heads should be bowed and all eyes closed. |
| Twelve | Always dress modestly as becomes Christians. |

# FOREWORD

Books are written with many intentions. However, the best books are written to provoke our thinking. **ALL RISE** is in that genre. If you read this book with agreement or disagreement in mind, you'll miss the point.

The essence is simple. The message is—mind your manners, you're in His house.

Dr. William E. Flippin Sr., Pastor of The Greater Piney Grove Baptist Church writes this book from years of careful observation of the erosion of church decorum.

Regardless of your church background, you do have standards. The corporate community calls it SOP (Standard Operating Procedures). These are relevant, communicated clearly, enforced rigorously for a reason—because, this defines corporate culture for that organization.

**ALL RISE** reminds and informs us that there is still need for *order in the church*.

Samuel R. Chand, D.D.
President, Beulah Heights Bible College
Atlanta, GA

# Dr. William E. Flippin, Sr.

*... "Again, The Kingdom of the Heavens is like a merchant in search of fine pearls; On finding one pearl of great value, he went and sold all that he had and bought it "... Matthew 13:46*

# BIO

The Reverend Dr. William E. Flippin, Sr. is a native of Nashville, Tennessee. His parents, Virginia and Richard Flippin recognized his leadership ability early in his childhood and encouraged him to succeed through education. He graduated with honors from Pearl High School in Nashville, where he served as president of the student body during his senior year. He furthered his education and earned a Bachelor of Arts degree in Mathematics and Business Administration from Fisk University in Nashville, graduating in 1974. In addition, he holds a Master of Divinity degree (Cum Laude) from Candler School of Theology at Emory University in Atlanta, Georgia; and a Doctorate of Ministry from McCormick Theological Seminary in Chicago, Illinois.

Among his many accomplishments, Dr. Flippin has distinguished himself by being named a Benjamin E. Mays Scholar for three years at Emory University; an inductee of the Morehouse College Board of Distinguished Preachers. He is on the Board of Trustees for the Morehouse School of Religion.

Faithfully serving as Senior Pastor of The Greater Piney Grove Baptist Church in Atlanta since 1990, Pastor Flippin has led The Greater Piney Grove to a unique sense of mission and outreach. The church has grown to a membership of over 7000 people. Each Sunday, three morning worship services speak of this pastor's vision for "equipping the saints." In his pastoral ministry, he has licensed and ordained over forty ministers and deacons. Under his leadership, Dr.

Flippin has added a staff to develop programs of fulltime ministry that serves the community and the world. In the fall of 1996, a multipurpose Family Life Center with more than 25,000 square feet of space was completed. This modern facility houses a gymnasium, child development center, bookstore, library, conference room and classrooms and is valued at almost $2,000,000. Reverend Flippin and The Greater Piney Grove family has also purchased over 30 acres of land for ministry expansion. The project is called 'The Promised Land.'

Dr. Flippin has been a pastor with distinction for two other historic churches in Georgia: Springfield Baptist Church, Greensboro, from 1980 – 1986; and Shoal Creek Baptist Church, Locust Grove, from 1986 – 1990. Occasionally, Pastor Flippin serves as visiting professor at Beulah Heights Bible College and Luther Rice Seminary. Dr. Flippin has had the honor of delivering the Baccalaureate Sermons at Fisk University (Nashville) and at Morehouse College (Atlanta).

Having a strong sense of community, Dr. Flippin serves on several community action committees and boards. In 1982, Dr. Flippin became an Associate in the

Department of Black Church Relations for the Georgia Baptist Convention. His primary role was to relate and establish joint cooperative religious activities between black and white Baptists in Georgia. In 1990, he was appointed to serve as a consultant for the convention and administers the Durward V. Cason Scholarship, which has a corpus of over $200,000. Additionally, Dr. Flippin serves as Board Chairman for Higher Plain Community Development, Incorporated, focusing on issues facing children and women in an economically diverse community.

He is the Board Chairman and CEO for **The Pearl Initiative, Inc** and **The Pearls of Great Price Ministries**. Dr. Flippin has been appointed by two Georgia Governors to serve on various state commissions. He was a delegate, from Dekalb County, to the National Democratic Party. He also serves as instructor for the National Baptist Congress of Christian Education; member of the Dekalb Chapter 100 Black Men; lifetime member of Alpha Phi Alpha Fraternity, Incorporated; and lifetime member of the NAACP. He conducts motivational and leadership workshops throughout the country and has traveled extensively to the Middle East while continuing to direct several programs that have allowed Baptists in Georgia to work together successfully.

Dr. Flippin has been married for almost thirty years to Sylvia Taylor, who is a high school mathematics instructor. Mrs. Flippin is a graduate of Vanderbilt University in Nashville and holds a Master's degree in Education from Georgia State University. For over ten years, Mrs. Flippin has taught in the Ministers' Wives Division for the National Baptist Congress of Christian Education and is an active member of Alpha Kappa Alpha Sorority.

Dr. and Mrs. Flippin are the proud parents of three sons and a daughter. William, Jr. is an ordained minister, a graduate of Morehouse College, Class of 1998 and a graduate of the Interdenominational Theological Center (ITC) with a Masters of Divinity degree. Recently, he received his Master of Theology degree from Candler School of Theology at Emory University in Atlanta, Ga. In the Fall of 2003, William will be pursuing his Ph.D. at Lutheran Theological Seminary in Chicago concentrating in Church History and Reformation Studies; Richard (Ricky) Curtis, is a graduate of Morehouse College, Class of 2001, He is a third year student at Candler School of Theology at Emory, he is also an ordain minister. For the past two summers, Richard has been the Summer Academy minister at Morehouse College. He will serve in this capacity in the Summer of 2004. Continuing the heritage,

(left to right): Joseph, William, Jr. & Richard.

Joseph Charles Taylor, an ordained minister, is a recent Cum Laude graduate of Morehouse College, Class of 2003, with a Bachelor of Arts degree in Political Science and Sociology. In the Fall of 2003, Joseph will

be attending Wesley Theological Seminary with a full scholarship. Their daughter, Sylvia Joi, is a high school student in the Fulton County School System and sings in the Greater Piney Grove Youth Choir.

(left to right): Sylvia Joi & Mrs. Sylvia Taylor Flippin

# INTRODUCTION

Creation came into existence through and by divine order. Where there is no order, the result is chaos and confusion. The Bible is clear that the devil is the author of chaos and confusion. The first book of Moses makes it clear that the earth was without form and void. It was a place of waste and emptiness. Darkness was upon the face of the deep. But the God who is light recreated himself and the darkness had to line up with the order of God. Light became day. For the next six days, God created the heavens, the earth, the firmament, the waters, the fish, the fowl, and even human life. In summation, God evaluated the progress and concluded that is was good. A noted Pastor in Indiana recently preached that the elements of creation must come to order. Nothing happens before it is time. God has a blueprint for our lives and this world. Even in what appears to be tension and turmoil, God still speaks and operates in order, and that which is nothing becomes something. Nothing means nothing to God. With God, all things are possible.

During my Christian experience beginning in Tennessee, I have seen the church and its people make some drastic changes. Many of the changes have been positive and productive. Some changes in the name of progress have resulted in a disconnected people with little in common.

It has been my privilege to serve as senior pastor of three great churches. Although the location, size and genre of each congregation were different, there remained a common need for leadership development.

Regularly, I hear ministers and church leaders express their concern that church members "do not know how to act in the church." Today, many sincere and very active members of our churches are first generation Christians. They have not been taught how to correctly act "churchy." Now this is both good and bad. Jesus warns us, and it is recorded in all of the synoptic gospels, that it is difficult to place new wine in old wine skins without causing a mess. On the other hand, some values and even church visionaries hate to use the word "tradition." Yet tradition has been lost due to the lack of a structured process of training and equipping the total church. Discipleship training is not something to be learned and mastered with a few seminars or retreats, nor can it be totally accomplished with a lengthy membership in a Sunday school class; it must be ongoing. The intent of this book is to clarify the need for order in the church.

I am hopeful that this will serve churches and ministers in other denominations, traditions and church structures. As all of us consider a calling on our lives, individually and collectively, we must have a clear understanding of our responsibility and roles. The harvest is plentiful, but the laborers are few. The preaching and sharing of God's Word and the leading of God's people must be done through the love of God. This work is written in love to encourage and to instruct. We are committed to believe that each church member, associate minister and leader in the local church will grow into a successful ministry. Many times young Christians and young ministers have complained to me that they were unsure of their roles and responsibilities. They have made mistakes, as we all will, and when they were chastised or corrected, they express that the error in worship or church etiquette was primarily due to a lack of instruction and training. In many of our churches, we have made minimal attempts to correct these errors by offering to teach church rules and behavior in youth retreats, church directories and new member orientation classes. None of these have gone quite far enough.

Leaders in churches want a class, a book or something as a written aid in church behavior and etiquette. After seven years, it becomes our challenge to look again at this whole area of decency and order in the church.

In my earlier work, I discussed that there is an unwritten church code of behavior that members are expected to know and understand; it is an unwritten "Ten Commandments." Have the tablets on which these commandments were written been ignored by the prophets and elders and broken on a rock, due to our continued disobedience? These rules, norms and expectations need to be clearly written. The prophet Habakkuk tells us that the vision should be made plain and written upon tables that we may run that readeth it. John Maxwell so eloquently says that everything rises and falls on leadership.

There must be order in the church and we, as church leaders, must implement and restore this order in our churches.

# THE STAGE IS SET

The contemporary church should not assume that individuals know what is expected and required for responsible church membership. We teach that the Holy Spirit will guide the believer into all truth; yet it is becoming more and more apparent that there is disorder and misbehavior in the body of Christ. Church members behave in a manner that does not add dignity and quality to the kingdom of God. There is a growing disrespect for the House of Worship and for those who serve the Lord's church and people.

For the last decade, the church has endured and survived despite adverse news of fallen leaders. Several ministers and ministries have been brought under the probing eyes of the world through the press. This bad publicity has caused an already skeptical society to justify their disrespect and dishonor of the church and the clergy. It is my belief that the historic resignation of Richard M. Nixon as President of the United States further resulted in a constant decline in admiration, respect, and reverence for leadership. All leaders are suspect to probes and questions. If you are a leader, you are assumed guilty until you prove your innocence. And even then, you have already been sentenced to a term of negativity, gossip, character assassination, and further distrust. People believe that leaders have ulterior motives and hidden agendas. This is evidenced as it becomes more difficult to get qualified individuals to run for public office. The scrutiny and sacrifice of privacy has caused caring and sincere persons not to enter the ministry and other public leadership roles. All of this has translated into a blatant disregard for the church and its leadership due to the poor example and error of a few.

Several years ago, an article in USA Today states the following: "Public trust and confidence in the federal government and the news media have declined dramatically since the Watergate break-in. Analysts say abuses of power uncovered by the Watergate probe that felled President Nixon caused Americans to become increasingly disillusioned with public institutions. However, attitudes toward the Watergate scandal itself have not changed. When Nixon resigned in 1974, 65% said that his infractions were serious enough to warrant his quitting. That number now is 68%. Over the past 25 years, trust and confidence has declined in:

- Congress from 71% to 54%
- the news media from 68% to 53%
- the presidency from 73% to 62%

Analysts say the media, eager to uncover more Watergates, lost public trust by overplaying scandal and government wrongdoing, often casting minor infractions as major exposes."

For quite some time, it has been my belief that the church has adopted the contemporary philosophy, that anything and everything is appropriate and deemed proper. With the adoption of "come as you are" and casual dress days in local churches, we have too often sent a signal that there are no boundaries of proper dress, conduct, or behavior for the contemporary Christian. We have "bought" into the notion and used to our personal advantage, that the Spirit of God gives us liberty. This liberty has been turned into an abused freedom. We have few, if any, limits required in our walk with Christ. Lackluster commitments produce divorce and consequently a society that has no real values or moral fiber.

This book will focus on church etiquette, leadership and order in the church. In lay terms, how do Christians act in church and in the world? What are the do's and don'ts of public worship? How do those who are not a part of the church perceive the church? What are we doing to help train those in the churches who have had no prior Christian experience? Have we taken too far the modern approach to church growth that allows people to "come as they are?" The Old Testament law is specific. Are there no limitations or guidelines for those who walk by faith and not by sight? What does grace require? Finally, is there any accountability for the way the Christian community behaves and is seen as a witness to the world? Are we so unlike other religions, which maintain a certain behavior for the world to observe or even emulate?

When I was a student in seminary, I enrolled in a course on ministerial etiquette. The instructor was Bishop Nolan B. Harmon. In the early 1980's Bishop Harmon was over ninety years old but still had a keen and insightful mind. Many students, actually expecting very little, registered for the class. What could this old man teach us young seminary students? Many of us were beginning pastors and had been raised in and around the church. We felt that certainly we knew all there was to know about the etiquette of ministers. Bishop Harmon had been one of the white ministers who drafted the letter written to Dr. Martin Luther King, Jr. when he was incarcerated in Birmingham, Alabama. Some leading white clergy in Birmingham wrote seeking to appeal to Dr. King's compassion and understanding that he might stop the protest and marches. They wanted him to resist the inhumane power of segregation with patient and passive resistance. History records that many tactics were used to dissuade blacks from boycotts and protest. Dogs and fire hoses were turned on the protesters as they marched in Birmingham for equality and justice.

Dr. King's response to these white clergy is known as "The Letter from the Birmingham Jail." Additionally, Bishop Harmon was also the editor of <u>The Interpreters Bible</u>. Many beginning pastors, like me, enrolled in this class feeling that we knew the proper conduct of being a minister. We felt this class would be an easy A. It would look good on our transcripts and help raise our overall grade point averages. To say the least, I have found myself, over 20 years later, often referring to the lectures of Bishop Harmon. As a result of this class and years of pastoral experience, I have felt the need to develop a handbook on Christian etiquette. Bishop Harmon used his wisdom and wealth of experience to challenge us, and much of what he taught was not in a text. He forced us to look at ourselves, to make certain that our lives, integrity, and character would not bring shame to the church and to the Christian ministry.

# THE NEED DEFINED

In many efforts to increase church attendance and membership, the church has adopted the ways and attitudes of the world. The late Dr. Martin Luther King, Jr. warned the church that we must be the headlights of the world, giving guidance, direction, and hope. He maintained that the church had become comfortable as the taillights to a world wandering in darkness.

It never ceases to amaze me that some members in the church have the attitude that church is the one place that nobody can tell them what to do. Many say, "It's my church and I pay my money. I can do what I want to in my church." I have observed that many of the local malls and shopping centers are full of young men and women walking around socializing. Many of the malls in our communities have become big weekend parties of walking, styling, and profiling for young and old. There is very little serious shopping, if any, taking place. The shopping mall has become the meeting and gathering place for our youth. Some have argued that this is good if it keeps them off the streets. Consequently, to keep the malls full, we allow people to gather who have no intentions of shopping. Likewise, to keep the schools full, we allow students to come to school with no books, no pencils, and no intention of learning. Also, to keep the church full, we allow men, women, boys and girls to come with no intention of worshiping or meeting God. In every instance, freedom has been taken to the extreme. Everybody can do his or her own thing. Something is drastically wrong with this and our world and our churches are suffering as a result.

Various circumstances will force a pastor, along the way, to make court appearances to provide character references, defense and support for one on trial. Each time I am called upon to provide this service, it causes me extreme and inexplicable anxiety. The security checks, the handcuffs, the weapons carried by the officers, and the heavy metal doors clanging and being locked as we are led from one area to the next, it is often too much for me to bear.

Yet the basis for the topic of this book comes from that very scene. Each time I enter a courtroom, there is order. To enter this massive room with a jury box, the court reporter's area, the defense table, the litigant's table, the flags which are symbols of the county, state, and nation, the bailiff and the judge's bench, causes almost a holy hush to all who enter. When the judge enters "those" huge doors, the bailiff does not ask, he demands with no warning, "All rise." Everyone jolts up and looks in the direction of the judge and we do not move until we hear the judge say: "You may be seated."

The judge wears a robe, the clergy wears a robe. The judge has authority backed by the law and government, the clergy has authority backed by the Word of God and the Holy Spirit. The judge speaks and all listen, the clergy speaks and all listen. The judge makes decisions that affect lives; the clergy makes decisions and delivers a gospel that affects lives.

So similar, so much alike. But I see an almost deliberate assault and attack to discredit and disrespect the authority, the decisions and the responsibility of the clergy and the church. If we would conduct ourselves in a court of law the same way we conduct ourselves in many of our churches, we would be immediately hushed out of the courtroom and charged with contempt of court. This is not so in most churches, it has, however, led to almost qualified and dignified disorder. If God placed divine order, even in the creation of life and living, then the church for which Christ died must have order. If God somehow would enforce this, many church leaders and members would be handcuffed and charged with contempt, confusion and disorderly conduct. There must be "Order in the Church."

# CHAPTER ONE

# Historical Markers

## *THE OPENING STATEMENT*

For over ten years, I had the honor of serving in the Department of Black Church Relations for the Georgia Baptist Convention. Many times I was called upon to intervene and manage church conflict. Further, I was called upon to provide leadership training and resources for churches that were growing or just beginning. Often conflicts would center on power struggles. Pastors would come for guidance because their ministry was hampered by constant battles of power. We must often work with church leaders and ministers who simply glory in a title and are not committed to the mission and ministry of the church. Likewise, disturbed and unsettled church leaders called upon our department for advice, guidance and comfort in their efforts and struggle to be useful partners in ministry. Many of the church members complained that their pastors were dictators, and pastors complained that their members were unwilling to change and grow. The primary cause for this conflict, I feel, lies in cultural patterns and traditions and often a lack of program and vision by pastors and church leaders. Vision, traditionally, has been noticeably absent in many of our churches. With these environmental factors in mind, the challenge was not to negate the past, nor allow the church to become a slave to it.

In culture, the masses of blacks have not been filled with self-worth and individual promise. Low wages, low expectations and low morals are conditions and myths placed upon blacks by the predominant culture. The black church provides a community wherein the people gathered, experience the truth of their lives as lived together in the struggle for freedom. Now, as in the past, the black church is all that some people can turn to and call their own. Sunday morning worship service, for the masses of black people, is still a gathering place for a people, who according to social status, are of little worth (maids, janitors, common laborers, and even corporate executives tainted by affirmative action.) These people become leaders in the church: senior female members are recognized as "head mothers," some men and increasingly women become highly respected deacons, while others assume roles varied as president of the church auxiliary and choir conductor. The pastor must struggle to be a leader by assisting these people to own a vision of the church and to possess the will to be kingdom builders. The pastor must not be dictatorial in the traditional sense of some churches. But many things in the black church will not change overnight. Deacons will continue to control some churches and some pastors will continue to be dictators. The black church seemingly places a great emphasis upon worship, and the importance of the preacher and sermon is central. Ideally, a people of God must be involved in partnership and participate in Sunday morning worship. A clear understanding of God's calling, purpose, and the significant need for all members in the body of Christ to be involved in ministry, will have positive results. In the context of the black church, the subdued and vocal people in society and even in the church must be challenged to identify and lift up common goals and a common mind. Individuality must be appreciated and each person must be encouraged to work toward fulfilling the mission of the church. This has both spiritual and social ramifications. Thus, a part of the Kingdom of God is actualized or made visible. This raises an intriguing challenge. The church is a community of believers who can freely share power and authority with and appreciate the work of all human beings. It is the role of the church for all who profess Christ to be equipped and encouraged to share their individual gifts for the edification of the whole.

### *Mission & Calling of the Black Baptist Church*

The black Baptist Church was born out of white Christianity's distortion of the gospel message in light of the concrete issue of slavery, particularly in the 18th and 19th century. Black Baptist lineage can be traced to a Virginian born slave named George Liele. Liele was emancipated and began traveling up and down the Savannah River (Georgia) preaching to slaves wherever friendly plantation owners would permit. He founded several churches before fleeing to Jamaica in 1783 fearing being placed back into slavery. Prior to this, he established black churches, some of which still exists. The white church for the most part was silent or provided theological legitimation for the slave codes and subsequent Jim Crow segregation laws. The theme of liberation is reflected in black culture that expresses black oppression and hopes for freedom through songs, dance, literature, poems, theatre and art. Then, the nature and calling of the black church is clearly defined. It is as an oppressed people of God formed by the creative power of God in the liberating work of Jesus Christ and the empowering of the Holy Spirit to become the free community of faith that participates in divine actions to create God's kingdom of free humanity in the world.

The starting point in developing the norm of liberation begins with the interpretation of the Bible. Most Baptists hold a literal understanding as a central doctrine. This discloses that God elected the Israelites in their oppressed condition, and is the ground of divine liberating activity in the struggles for freedom. The theophany at Sinai (Exodus 19:4-5b) points to the politics of God who chooses an oppressed community of faith, reaffirms the Abraham covenant with them (Genesis 17:6-8), and eventually enables them to possess a land. The writer in this context articulates their hurts and hopes in the struggle for liberation. This is further amplified in Israelite prophecy that reveals Yahweh's concern for justice within the community as an example to all nations. This is echoed in the heart of the ancient prophet Amos' preaching (Amos 5:24). Thus, Yahweh is disclosed in the Old Testament as the God of the oppressed who is involved in the struggle for freedom and human dignity.

Jesus reaffirms the theme of liberation in grounding the purpose of his ministry in Isaiah's proclamation (Luke 4:18, 19). The mission and calling of the black church is closely related to these scriptural themes. Christian scriptures, therefore, articulate the faith of two oppressed faith communities, namely Israel and the New Testament Church, whose freedom is inextricably bound to the divine economy operative in human liberation as fully disclosed in Jesus Christ.

This writer has had a perception of mission and ministry that has been primarily limited to that of the black minister and the black church. In my Christian and social community, as well as in most black communities, the ministerial profession was the first and almost only one to gain a foothold in the community. Not only does it have historical precedence and prominence and involve disinterested service, but it also has a divine sanction. This combination of factors made and makes the black preacher (minister) supreme among black leaders. The noted black scholar, W. E. B. DuBois, wrote:

*The black preacher is the most unique personality developed by blacks on American soil. He is a leader, a politician, an orator, a "boss", an intriguer, an idealist—all these qualities the black clergy possesses.*

*(DuBois, 1903, p. 190).*

Throughout my ministerial journey, I have struggled to fit into the norm or the place society and especially the black community has designated for the black minister. Yet, in being the "boss", as set forth by

DuBois, I often preached and ran "my" church with an iron hand. While making the effort to maintain peace and loyalty among the parish members and the surrounding community, I could recognize no sense for service and no effort or spirit of joint mutuality, partnership, and cooperation (between clergy and laity) to fulfill the work and life of the church of Christ. In my personal development and growth, with theological, biblical, and spiritual maturity, I continue to struggle with becoming more acutely aware that the church we serve is not "my" church but the church of Christ.

Ephesians 4 says that the pastor is called to equip the saints, not boss them. Nor can the pastor or church leaders alone do the work of the church. Therefore, the mission of the church, and not just the pastor, must be to get the uninvolved involved. With this in mind, leadership takes a totally revolutionary focus for most black churches. The mission of the black church is involving people to do things for themselves. Efforts to win approval and support for church programming by doing everything single-handedly will ultimately lead to defeat.

## Partnership and Leadership in the Black Baptist Church

Leadership style is very strong and extremely important in the black Baptist Church. The leader is highly respected and even feared, as is a judge who leads his or her courtroom. This traditional manner or emphasis of polity in black church leadership has historical beginnings after slavery when most churches worshiped part-time and the pastor only came to the church bi-weekly or monthly. The church existed with few long-term programs of ministry. The deacons or a group of hand picked leaders were charged at that time with almost the total care and nurture of the church the remainder of the month. The pastor was required to preach, conduct funerals and weddings. The length and even subject matter of the sermons were often dictated by these church leaders. The power of the deacons was concentrated, static, stable, unchanging, and traditional.

It is sad to say that many black churches in our nation are still operating in this manner. Again, it is because of a cultural pattern and a lack of programming and vision. More recently, however, with a more trained clergy who devote full-time service to the local church, pastors have developed more clearly into leadership, executive and administrative roles. The pastor, like no one else, is generally held responsible for the total life and work of the church. This produces, as Robert Worley says in a class I attended on The Theory of Organizational Behavior, pastors who are marketers of religion. Church growth is equated with numbers and quality of life. The contemporary black minister must become more than a dictatorial manager; he or she must also be involved in the calling back, the reminding, and the calling out of those in the body of Christ to our purpose and mission. The calling of the black pastor is to utilize every member in the life of the church so that there is ownership as we build a people of God in a gathered community called the body of Christ. This becomes a collection of people where everyone's contribution is welcomed and expected. A concern for the "whole" community, world, and even the self must be stressed in this project. Encouraging members to embrace corporate ministry will enable them to think and feel about themselves in a new way.

Martin Buber's work contains some important lessons about biblical leaders (Buber, 1968, 141ff). Buber warns that it is often the weak and humble who are chosen to lead. The choice of the younger sons to carry the promise is a good case in point. Abel, Jacob, Joseph, Moses, and David fall into this category. Buber also recalls that God's purpose is fulfilled not by might, nor by power, but "by my Spirit" (Zechariah 4:6). As Buber remarks, biblical leaders are leaders only in so far as they allow themselves to be led by the Spirit of God.

Closely tied to the black church's comprehension of the black pastor is Buber's understanding of the leader, and the example is Moses. This leader is one who guides the wandering people of God. Indeed, without this leader, there would be no people as such. An important quality of leadership implied here is that the leader forms and guides a people who are looking for direction.

Like our judicial system which is aimed at protecting the laws of the state, municipality, and the rights of others, the black church traditionally had to serve as an extended family for a people whose own foundational core of family and security could be removed at a moment's notice. Dulles (1974:51ff) refers to this as mystical communion. The black pastor or deacon has been given "all power" in the polity of the black Baptist

Church. This is closely tied to traditional beliefs of these leaders as shepherd or father figures. Another example can be found in an organization in the black Baptist church known as the Mother's Board in which certain women who are generally elderly serve as role models for the church. The critical point of this church structure is that it leads to exclusiveness with stress on a special class of church members with privileges that others do not possess in the church. The black Baptist church must further expand and allow all members of the church to feel a part of the church family. More importantly, they can, as the people of God, provide input in the total life of the church. This addresses the need to identify and be a part of a larger family of Christian believers who gather for worship on Sunday. Although some of this is not exclusively a part of the black Baptist church, it does serve as historical and traditional method of inclusion especially for these people who feel otherwise disinherited all week long.

# CHAPTER 2

# A PRACTICAL GUIDE TO BEHAVIOR IN THE BLACK CHURCH

## *THE CHARGES AND CLAIMS*

Dr. Martin Luther King, Jr. said in an interview in 1965 that we (blacks) have to face and live with the fact that the Negro has not developed a sense of stewardship. Slavery was so divisive and brutal, so molded to break up unity, that we never developed a sense of oneness. Starting with the individual family unit, the black in slavery, separated families from families, and the pattern of disunity that we among Negroes today derive from this cruel fact of history (Washington, 1986, page 369). This definitely has and will continue to have an effect on the recording and keeping of church history.

Among the most difficult habits to break for the white master was the slaves' tenacious hold on the value they placed on the folktale. Any method to destroy strong African roots was the slave-master's way to divide and conquer. Further, the use of folktales is most definitely seen today in the importance of the sermon in the black Baptist Church. The folktales, during slavery, were true to the structure and motif of their African prototypes. A significant number of African folktales appear to be stories and myth about animals, such as lions, elephants, and monkeys (Carruthers, 1986, pg 2).

Prosecutors and defense lawyers are trained to story-tell – a masterful art to learn. The art of story telling is persuasive and helps to convey the message of the case to a jury or judge. Similarly, the art of story telling has always been extremely important in the black church. Often a person in the "amen corner" in the black church encourages the preacher by exclaiming, "tell the story." In <u>Models of the Church</u>, Dulles maintains that this is an example of the church as herald (1974, page 81f.) The great majority of us live by a story that has been handed down to us and often becomes a strong symbol which affects our notion about God and the church. These stories need to be incorporated in such a way that the church history is recorded. Further, skills in the writing of that history must be learned.

As stated earlier, in the black Baptist Church, the development and performance of ministry has largely been the sole task of the pastor. This has historical and social precedence in the black community. When this leader is absent, the Board of Deacons makes decisions, controls, and sets the tone of ministry. Sometimes the sharing of power is offered minimally to a few members of the congregation. But, if God's people are called from bondage and oppression into a place of freedom, then the church is called to be free and to set at liberty those who are oppressed. Much of black church history is lost because people feel they are not a part of the whole. Their stories, experiences and perspectives are discounted because they are not a part of "the group." The "priesthood of all believers" provides a model for partnership and mutuality which the church should manifest. Within the church, this will mean willingness to share power and conduct ministry in non-oppressive ways. If black Baptists believe in the "priesthood of all believers" then, the planning and performance of ministry and even the writing of church history will be a shared task of clergy and laity alike. It will not be the specific task of a select few or an individual. The church, in its very nature, must be a people "called of God" in forming and shaping ministry. The spirit of the black Baptist Church will be one of partnership in ministry. The sharing of power to decide, construct and implement the ministry of the church will be the task of the entire church.

One of the primary objectives of the black Baptist Church is to help the congregation members to feel a part of the whole work of the church. Further, these efforts should lead the church in participatory ministry and utilize the present gifts of the church. Church history will be freely shared and recorded when the expectations and participation of members is changed from a clergy or deacon-led congregation to a body of Christ led by the people of God.

Several clergy and church members have shared with me that they have observed members who have stopped by the area's fast food restaurants. They bring sausage biscuits, French fries and other food items into the sanctuary to feed *Junior* because it was too early for him to get up and eat. Some people use the sanctuary as a cafeteria. For months now, we have been forced to place in our Sunday bulletin a request for worshipers not to eat in the sanctuary. Food and refreshments served during church services have been used as a reward to keep *Junior* quiet. Many rules for raising children in the past have been replaced with more modern techniques. Nevertheless, when I was a child in church, I would get disciplined in church as readily as at home. Often, the discipline did not come from my parents, but from the adults closest to me at the time of my misbehavior. They would tell my parents that they had to speak to me about my behavior. Consequently, I would be in trouble all over again with my parents.

Several persons have gone to convenience stores near churches and purchased soft drinks, chips, cookies, and candies. They eat while at worship, at choir rehearsal, and at prayer meetings. It seems that at least they would take the trash from their *"pew picnic"* to the nearest wastebasket. But instead, it is left behind with the attitude that the church janitor is paid to pick up the trash. It is not my intention to deceive you. As a young boy, my friends and I would hold back some of our *Sunday School* offering, sneak out of church and visit the nearby store. But we did have the decency to eat our purchases **before** we came back into church.

My brother, who is a pastor in Tennessee, and his son, does upholstery. Recently, they received a contract to cover the pews of a church in their city. He shared with me that he and his son retrieved from the old pews a large bucket of chewing gum stuck to the bottom of the pews. From the old covers, they found the remnants of piecrusts, crumbs, and other items. Once, a janitor at our church found a lottery ticket and wrapper used for cocaine in the hymnal rack. The matter of respect for the Lord's house is at an all time low. This trend must be addressed, changed and not tolerated. During the welcome period in the church, we hear too often an invitation to the visitor and members to *sit back and relax.* It is no time to relax when things are getting worse. There is a struggle for us to address this breakdown in structure.

When my family and I have vacationed, we have toured some of the magnificently structured cathedrals. Every place we toured, there were clearly indicated areas where one could go and others that were marked "off limits." Certain areas were held with honor and respect.

People do not have the attitude, even as a tourist, that *I have paid my money on this tour, and can walk anywhere I please.* When we toured some of the great church buildings and cathedrals, I was always struck with envy by the manner in which those who would go on these tours spoke quietly and with respect. These places, many times, have persons praying and lighting candles. Yet the tours do not distract the worshipers from their religious activities. On the other hand, as we observe many of our churches, we see the exact opposite. Many of our churches are now on cable television and provide a valuable service of broadcast and outreach. Yet, it is quite disturbing to observe people talking and chewing gum. Many times, choir members, in obvious view of the camera, are talking and looking uninterested in the service (except for the musical portion of the service.) Recently, I was observing worship service on cable television and saw a person seated behind the pulpit area yawning and stretching as if he had just awakened from a night's sleep. Such behavior would not be tolerated in a court of law and may result in a reprimand from the judge or bailiff. Our members must be taught that their decorum and dignity in worship is of critical importance. Too often, worship is a time of entertainment rather than a time of introspection.

My wife made a keen observation as we were on a travel tour during our annual summer vacation. When the hotel personnel instructed us to be at the departure site at a certain time, all who paid their fares were present. The schedule was kept very tight. No one broke the rules or procedures. My wife also noted that all the travelers were cooperative, even though they had paid their money for the tour.

During a tour last summer of the Pearl Harbor Memorial, we were shuttled to the area in a small boat.

The official from the Navy said, "While traveling to the USS Arizona Memorial site, you are welcome to take pictures but remain seated." He continued, "You are under the jurisdiction of the United States Navy, and we will ask you to leave the boat if any Navy guidelines are violated." Needless to say, I sat with disbelief at the level of complete cooperation of these tourists compared to that of church members. Why did no one protest? Most were U.S, citizens, and many were taxpayers. All of us, however, had paid our entrance, transportation, and tourist fees. No one protested because we knew that if we did not follow the rules, we would be *put off the boat.* If a minister had made a similar statement to church members and visitors during a worship service, we would be met with angry protests and threats to join another church. If churches would expect and demand certain behavior in the church, many of the problems presented so far in this work would be alleviated.

If the leaders would band together and demand respect for the House of God, these things would change. *While a person is in and under the jurisdiction of the church, misbehavior must not be tolerated just for popularity and fame.*

As mentioned earlier, the model for behavior in the church must be accepted as a serious responsibility of the leadership of the church. The pastor, officers, auxiliary and ministry leaders must take the lead in what is proper church behavior. We must believe and lift up to the people, "follow me as I follow Christ." We must teach by example that there must be order in the church. While never forgetting that the Spirit of God is present, there must be certain acceptable decorum. God had divine order when the world was created. The animals were not created before there was light. The fish of the sea did not come before the waters of the deep leaped forth from the lips of God. Some "spiritual" folk criticize churches that have an Order of Worship. The Order of Worship is a guide, not a yoke of bondage. The Holy Spirit must always be allowed to alter and modify the worship, but even the Holy Spirit does things decently and in order.

One of the reasons church etiquette has gone lacking in recent years stem from ending training union programs. Years ago, most churches and denominations held a Sunday afternoon of weekly training program. The Baptists had *Baptist Training Union* (BTU). At its inception, this was called the

*Baptist Young Peoples Union* (BYPU). This was the training ground for the young, the responsibly involved church member, and the adult leader. The Methodist Church, Church of God in Christ, and the Catholic Church had fellowships or unions, which primarily taught church behavior, doctrine procedure, order and etiquette. It was in the Baptist Training Union hour in my home church, that we were taught how to properly read scripture, when it was proper to walk in and out of the church worship service, and how to address the pulpit when giving a welcome address or making public remarks. We were also taught how to pray. In other words, we were taught how to behave in church. It was in the training union that the hard questions were dealt with openly and honestly.

This guide will serve the local churches in the training of its members. There are twelve points that have been presented for your consideration.

## *POINT ONE*

*BE ON TIME. You need at least five minutes after your arrival at the church building to get prepared for worship. Even if you are attending a committee meeting, it must always be seen as an opportunity for worship. Arrive early to compose your body and mind to be sensitive to the HOLY SPIRIT and to whisper a prayer before the service begins.*

I was always taught that one takes care of personal needs and conducts church business matters before entering the sanctuary for worship. Some seem to think that the bathroom facilities in the church are closed and are not in operation until the organist begins playing the prelude. Parents must teach their children that, just as in school, in the church there are times for breaks and recesses. Teachers do not allow students to get up during the class period and excuse themselves. I hear so often that many are taking medicine and must be excused. But many that are excusing themselves have not been to a doctor in years. Many have admitted to me that they were responding to beepers, socializing, or just taking a stretch break. A great deal of unnecessary walking around would end if the rules of yesteryear were followed today. That is, all personal needs should be attended to before the worship begins.

One must arrive at the House of God early and on time. Too many of our churches have misrepresented or PUBLICIZED and even advertised that worship begins at 10:45 a.m., and yet we consistently begin late or when a certain number have people arrived. I am not advocating becoming a slave to the clock, but we must respect timeliness.

## POINT TWO

*Never pass up the aisle during prayer or scripture reading.* If you must be excused, your presence and movement will distract and draw attention away from the pulpit. Therefore, take great pains to leave as quietly as possible.

During the invitational period, no unnecessary walking should be allowed. This is an eternal time. Souls are hanging in the balance of salvation and damnation. Be very sensitive to the moving of the Holy Spirit during this time of worship.

## WHEN NEVER TO WALK IN CHURCH

*During the Invitation to Discipleship;*

*During the reading of the Scripture;*

*During prayers for any occasions;*

*During the baptism or the Lord's Supper;*

*During the message*

When the bailiff announces the entrance of the judge, all in the courtroom must cease movement and stand with respect, in honor of the judge's entrance. Similarly, while praying, all walking and movement must cease. Just as a bailiff controls the entrances and exits of a courtroom, an usher should close doors and turn toward the pulpit area to also join in the period of prayer. Please note that one prayer is no more important than another. One person who has the reputation of "praying heaven down" must not be respected more than the one who prays for what we term "a less significant prayer." For instance, most of us pay little attention to the offertory prayer because it is short, brief, and generally lacks the emotion of an altar prayer. But in many of our churches, the devotional or altar prayer commands greater attention and respect. **Prayer is prayer,** irrespective of when it is given and for what purpose.

When Jesus read in the temple from the book of Isaiah, the bible states all eyes were fixed upon Him. I think this is an excellent point of observation and comparison. When the word of God is read, all eyes, all hearts, and all ears should be turned in the direction of the reader of the Word. Some churches require worshippers to stand whenever the scripture is read. More and more people are bringing their Bibles to church and welcome the calling of their attention to the Word of God. Definitely, when scripture is read, all other activity should stop.

When you are asked to participate in the worship service, you should stand, do what is asked of you and then be seated. If you are asked to read the scripture, you do not have to make opening remarks. If you do a special announcement, do not preach a mini-sermon. If you are asked to pray, please do not make remarks or give a testimony. The words of welcome should not be a time of exhortation and personal agendas. I have requested people to pray during the offertory period, during which they never mention or bless the offering. Can you imagine a person praying grace over a meal and never mentioning the food? The point is to do the task you are called on to do. Of course, the Holy Spirit can alter any assignment. The tragedy is that we often blame the spirit when our real intent is "getting something off our chests."

To add to this point, when the invitation is extended for salvation and church membership, no one should be moving except (1) the ministers, (2) church officers assisting in the invitation, and (3) those moving forward in response to the invitation and call to discipleship. To walk or divert attention from the invitational period will always be a distraction. None would want a sinner not to accept Christ as Lord and Savior due to church member's inappropriate behavior during the most critical period of worship. We must be more serious about soul winning.

In this same vein, it is essential that as soon as the invitation period has ended, worshippers do not make a mad dash for the exit doors. To act in this manner, one misses the benediction and may cause a person to miss the opportunity for a meaningful church experience to end properly. The end of worship is always the benediction. The benediction is the blessing upon the people for a productive week of Christian life and witness.

Do not use the invitation to Christian discipleship period to walk, talk, greet, get to know, or meet someone, or even go to the restroom. This is the most serious and meaningful part of the service. This may be the last time a man, woman, boy or girl will have a chance to accept Jesus as his Lord and personal Savior. If you are not sure what to do or when to do it, an usher should be able to direct you.

*James 1:5-8*        *Colossians 4:2-6*

*Deuteronomy 4:29-30*

Finally, a further distraction during the worship service is reading the church bulletin or newsletter while the choir is singing or a minister is speaking. Visitors to our churches have expressed that in many of our churches, they are absolutely annoyed and insulted by the manner in which persons who profess to be mature Christians act and react in and out of the church. While sitting in church, some church members are commenting on everything, conversing with other members, writing notes and reading the hymnal, Bible, or dong other things. These may cause one to miss making contact with God in the worship service. I have observed that persons participating in these distractions often do so when there is friction, disrespect, or dislike toward the person speaking or performing.

## POINT THREE

*Be respectful of the worship service.* If the sermon has begun, take a seat near the door. This applies even if you are in your home church and familiar with the seating arrangements. Ministers must never walk into the pulpit after the service has begun unless invited by the pastor to participate. Visiting deacons should be seated, as are all other worshipers. In most cases, deacons and ministers will be identified and invited by the persons in charge. Always be willing to participate in the service after being recognized.

Often ushers are seated after the minister announces the text for the sermon. Churches that have multiple services and other activities simultaneously occurring during Sunday morning worship may want to rethink this approach. Ushers who are assigned to the doors leading into and out of the sanctuary should remain on post at the door during the sermon. This insures that anyone entering the worship after the sermon has begun is led to specific seats.

Do not walk down the aisle looking for your *special seat* after the worship begins, unless the ushers lead you to that seat. On this same note, when a worshipper becomes ill in church or moves in any way during the sermon, all eyes and attention will be directed toward that individual. The handling of these concerns should be done quickly, quietly, and with as little fanfare as possible to avoid the worshipers being drawn away from the minister and the message. If the worship service has begun and you arrive late, please be seated as close to the door as possible. No minister should ever WALK INTO THE PULPIT after the sermon has begun. Moreover, if you are expected to serve in the

pulpit ministry, you should arrive at the church early.
Our church has over 40 licensed or ordained ministers.
There are only ten seats in the pulpit. So each Sunday,
some of the ministers must sit in the pews. We do ask,
however, that a minister sit near the front whenever
possible. At times during the year, deacons and
ministers may sit and worship with their families and
not be in an official capacity each Lord's Day.

## POINT FOUR

*Be devout in every attitude.* All whispering should be
studiously avoided. Share your hymnal and Bible with
your neighbor. If you are visiting a church, always
conform to its custom of worship.

At times it becomes necessary to speak a word to a
neighbor or an usher. I have observed members of
churches carrying on lengthy and detailed
conversations. Some have even turned their entire
bodies toward the person to whom they were talking. It
becomes obvious to all around, but gets worse rather
than ceases. Sometimes the pastor may wonder if he is
being too observant when these conversations take

place during the worship service. But recent videotaping of worship services and choir concerts have confirmed that some adults are worse than the children in respect to talking during the entire church service. The polite step to take when someone keeps talking in church during the worship service is to say, "Excuse me, but we can continue this conversation after church." To converse with an individual in the church looks bad; it is rude and disrespectful to the speakers or worship leaders.

Several months ago, I attended a church where a deacon was making change and counting the money on the communion table. Once upon a time, no one touched or moved the communion table except for a wedding or funeral. This table was honored, most revered and almost worshiped. We were made to feel that if we touched it or dishonored it in anyway, a bolt of lightning would strike us dead. Perhaps, we may have carried this too far, but we should respect this piece of church furnishing and *all* church furnishings and property.

# POINT FIVE

## Be thoughtful of the comfort of others.

Take the center of the pew from each side, if you are the first to enter. Leave all vacant space at the end next to the aisle for those who will need to be seated after your arrival.

The worship leaders and leaders of the church must first be the example of the servant. The minister should always display a servant spirit. Jesus has set the example. He came to serve – not to be served. We have lost common courtesy for others. Men disrespect women. The young disrespect the elders. The "haves" disrespect the "have-nots" and vice versa.

When I moved to Atlanta, I was riding the new MARTA (Metropolitan Atlanta Rapid Transit Authority) system. Upon reaching my destination, I transferred to a city bus. The bus was full and people were standing in the aisles while traveling through downtown Atlanta. A gentleman (at least I thought he was), who was seated, noticed a woman standing next to him in the aisle. After he offered her his seat, the woman cursed this man and told him how degrading he had made her feel. She loudly protested, stating that she was humiliated by his arrogant display and that he must feel that she was too fragile to stand. All of us were appalled, shocked, hurt and dismayed that the world had come to this point.

Again allow me to address those who come into the worship service and stake claim to certain seats. It is unchristian and inconsiderate. This is especially wrong when you set anchor at the end of the pew and everyone must crawl over you to be seated. I have seen church members who have seats claimed, and they look at people who move into that row as if to say, "I shall not be moved; like a tree planted, I shall not be moved." A server must be willing to give up his seat for another.

Finally, if one prefers a certain seat and the sanctuary fills quickly with worshipers, one needs to arrive early to assure a seat of preference. Reserved seating needs to be kept to a minimum. One cannot feel that he is the proprietor of a seat or pew.

If you know that you must leave the worship early

or if you need to take medicine, do not sit in the first three rows of the church on Sunday morning or during worship service or auxiliary meetings. You will distract the congregation as you come and go.

*Psalm 27:4*          *Habakkuk 2:20*

*Psalm 25:8-11*

Please do not draw attention by raising your hand and pointing your index fingers in the air (as you excuse yourself). Where did this practice begin in our churches? A little boy asked me one day as a sister was leaving church, "Why is that lady telling us that she is number one?" This is a bad habit and only draws attention.

If you are aware that your children have the tendency to misbehave or fuss during worship service, preventing everyone from hearing and being blessed by the worship time, do not sit on or near the front row.

*Deuteronomy 6:1-9*          *Proverbs 22:6*

Don't allow your children to cry for fifteen minutes

during church services and activities before deciding that they are not going to stop crying. Church ushers should swiftly assist parents when this occurs.

*James 3:17*        *Ephesians 1:17*

Don't allow your children to tear up the pew Bible, or draw funny faces in the hymnals in an attempt to keep them quiet or busy during the Sunday morning service.

*Proverbs 3:1-6, 11-12*        *Proverbs 13:24*

Don't allow your children to run all around and through the church. They should not be allowed to roam freely around the church without supervision. This includes the church grounds, sanctuary, and during auxiliary meetings and choir rehearsals. The church represents the House of God. We are not to do certain things in respect of the House of God, regardless of age.

*Isaiah 28:9-10*        *Isaiah 54:13*

If you must chew gum during church services, it would look much better in your mouth than under the church pews.

## POINT SIX

*Speak a bright cheery word to as many as possible. Do not draw attention to yourself or to the conversation you may hold with another. Many churches have a period during the worship and after the service for hearty and joyful fellowship.*

*Being friendly is always a drawing card to visitors. If you are sitting near visitors introduce them to the pastor or to some of the church officers. Make certain you get their names and call them during the week to invite them back to your church.*

There is nothing worse than going to church and meeting unfriendly people. The church should always be a place where people come and participate willingly. Personal agendas, attitudes, and business concerns of the previous week should take a second place to worship, preaching, and the saving of souls. The pastor can preach the best sermon, the choir could sing until heaven falls, and the facilities could be immaculate and modern, but an unfriendly member can inspire negative attitudes about the church among visitors. This is critical as many visitors do not return to the church because of some unkind Spirit or attitude of a member that ought to know and do better. People sometimes act as if they are mad with God, mad with the pastor, mad with the church, and mad with life. If the real truth were told, they are mad at themselves.

## *POINT SEVEN*

*Properly address the pulpit and church body.* When a member comes before the church to address the body of Christ, there must be order. Some have made light of the manner in which the African American church recognizes those seated in the pulpit and the honored leaders of the church. Yet, the older I become, the more sense it makes to me that it is rude to enter another person's house and never recognize them. Can you imagine someone knocking on your door at your home and, when you open the door, they just walk in, sit down where they please, and say nothing. You would wonder if they lacked basic home training and courtesy.

The following guidelines should be observed when standing before the church or a church gathering:

- First give reverence (honor) to God. God gets first place in all things.

- Then honor and recognize the pastor. This should be done even if the pastor is absent.

- It is proper to recognize the pastor's spouse. Without them, much of the pastor's success would not occur.

- Recognize the Reverend Clergy. You may briefly note and recognize some of the clergy, ministers, or local dignitaries who have earned high honor and respect. Please be mindful that once we begin to call names and make special recognitions, we will probably offend some that feel they also deserve this honor and recognition.

- Recognize the official boards of the church, for they stand with the pastor in the success of the church and ministry;

- Recognize the Mother's boards and other officials/ leaders in the church;

- Finally, recognize the brothers and sisters or members and visiting friends.

Further, it is polite for the congregation, the ministers, and the officers to answer the greetings with "Amen." Many hearty and spirited greetings in the church are dampened when the speaker says, "Good morning, church" and receive no reply. The speaker feels defeated before he or she begins the second sentence. Whenever addressed, I always say thank you aloud for the person to hear and know I appreciate their respect and honor.

This matter has nothing to do with worshiping the creature over the creator. Some who are bitter argue that this is unnecessary and shows too much admiration for men and women. But I take liberty to use again the illustration that it is unchristian and unkind to come into the home of a person and not respect or recognize the leader (head) of the house.

Some of us would be better Christians, better choir members, ushers, trustees, presidents, or deacons if we didn't have to have so much credit for what we do for the Lord and the church.

*Psalm 84*          *Matthew 5:16*

*Proverbs 28:1-5 13*

People with evil dispositions, ugly personalities, and who rarely have anything to smile about, should not serve on the Usher Ministries, Welcome Committees, or sit in the choir loft or pulpit.

*Romans 12:1-10*          *I John 4:7-11*

*Colossians 3:12-17*

## POINT EIGHT

***Never put on your coat or wrap during the closing hymn. Do not make a rush for the door immediately after the benediction is pronounced.***

*Likewise, the Church parking lot should be a place to show Christian courtesy and patience.*

Don't use the Sunday service when the junior or youth ushers are on duty to walk in and out of the church. Though there are young people at the door and standing to assist throughout the church, they also deserve our respect. When the junior ushers are in uniform, they are in a position of authority. This authority stands, regardless of their age. If a person wants respect from others, he or she first must give it.

*Deuteronomy 6:4-9*       *Psalm 26:4-5*

*Proverbs 25:28*

Some choir members can't wait until they finish the last song before they start tipping and sneaking out the back door.

*Ecclesiastes 7:1-14*       *Luke 8:4-15*

## POINT NINE

*There should be no loud talking or jesting after the service is concluded.* This is always out of order. Go to an individual privately and never talk loudly or be involved in fault-finding with another.

## POINT TEN

*Let Reverence be the keyword.* The church must demand this often neglected quality. If the worship and the House of God are to be respected, they must be honored at all times. The presence of the Lord must be honored at all times.

It is an honor when a church ordains or appoints an individual as a deacon of the church. It must be noted, however, that the person is a deacon only in the church where he is ordained or appointed. If a deacon is a visitor in the church, he is to sit in the pews, as do all other worshipers. If the deacon is recognized by one of the church leaders and then invited to the front or to a designated seat, then and only then should the deacon come forward. Likewise, licensed ministers have been recognized as having a gift and calling from God by their local church. Thus, they are deacons and ministers at their local church only.

## POINT ELEVEN

*During prayer, all heads should be bowed and all eyes closed.* Say "AMEN" during and at the end of the prayer. Say "AMEN" to the preached word to encourage and to witness to the truth of God's word. The polite and sincere nodding of one's head is no substitute for making a joyful noise unto the Lord.

Say "amen" to the sermon and during the worship services. Many have attempted to excuse themselves from this verbal response with the nodding of the head. Too many of our churches have adopted a style of worship that is more conducive to a good nap than spirit-filled worship. Though these may be sincere gestures, the Scripture says, "Let the redeemed of the Lord say so."

The worship time is not the period to do a critical

analysis of the singing, the sermon, or the prayers. I have seen people sit in church with pen or pencil circling errors and misprints in the bulletin. Many times they are noting whenever a verb is misused or a word mispronounced, and each time a note is missed in the song or on the musical instrument. These individuals miss the whole meaning and purpose of worship. Generally, these individuals are miserable people. And misery loves company. The Spirit of the Lord comes when the church is on one accord. When the church prays and seeks God's face, then will we hear from heaven? Many of our churches never experience God because "that which is flesh is flesh but that which is spirit is spirit."

Through the years, I have seen ministers who sit in the worship with sour faces and who never gave a hint of encouragement to the minister who is preaching. Of course, the exception to this is, if they personally like the minister, then that makes the word of God they *preach more real.* Isn't it time to cease this foolishness? "Be not deceived, whatsoever one sows that he shall also reap." I have seen ministers who sit with others and refuse to participate in the preaching process.

What goes around comes around. The most critical persons in the church are often hiding their own personal insecurities. They criticize others, but they can never themselves reach the same mark or achievements of the person they criticize. No, I am not advocating that you be a pulpit or pew cheerleader for the sake of noise. However, just as you encourage the child who is learning or attempting to do his/her best, so should brothers and sisters encourage each other.

Perhaps one may not be the best preacher. Perhaps, the choir may not be the best in town, singing the top ten. Nevertheless, an encouraging "amen," a friendly smile, and a positive response will often lift up the service and the participants in the worship. Don't sit in the church being so spiritual that you may be guilty of missing the SPIRIT when He comes.

When one is encouraged in preaching, one preaches better. This is the beauty of the African-American church. God tells Jeremiah, "Do not be hindered in your ministry by the look on their faces."

A word to ministers: Ministers should always have a good and wholesome relationship with their pastor and church members. When a minister is being considered at another church for the pastor or staff member, he or she should not do so in secret. In every case, the pulpit committee, the officers and the members of the new church will call the church of his/her membership for a reference. If a minister is not cooperative and does not have a good relationship with the pastor and the church, it is unlikely that, as a pastor, the same minister would have good relationships with deacons, officers and members of the church he or she seeks to lead.

It is sad and disheartening to see our leaders sitting on the front row sleeping or resting their eyes during Worship Service. It suggests, especially to children and guests, that what is happening is neither important nor interesting – so wake me when it is over.

*Matthew 26:40-46     John 4:19-24*

*Proverbs 25:25-28*

Some people, because of who they are, are placed in charge of seminars, workshops and lecture series, but haven't been to Sunday school or Christian education sessions in years.

*II Timothy 2:15     John 5:39*

## POINT TWELVE

*Always dress modestly as becomes Christians.*
Perhaps we have saved the most controversial matter
for last. The whole discussion of proper dress and
attire is a long-standing debate in the body of Christ.
Some churches do not allow the women to wear
makeup, open-toe shoes, pants/slacks and short
dresses. One of the great and unfortunate things about
many of these rules and regulations is that they are
often directed at women and are almost always
unbiblical.

One wonderful thing about this discussion is the
ongoing debate concerning the wearing of uniforms in
public schools. Private and parochial schools have long
followed this practice. All over this country, we are
hearing reports of young men and women losing their
lives because their clothes are stolen off their backs.
Designer labels and expensive jewelry have further
aggravated this situation. As a parent, I know that
tennis shoes, jackets and brand named clothing are
expensive.

Peer pressure forces most people to buy what we

don't need, to impress folk we don't like, with money we don't have. Peer pressure is also in the church. All of us have heard people excuse themselves from worship because they do not have the proper clothes to wear.

In the wardrobe of every minister, church officer or lay leader, there needs to be a black suit or dress with a white shirt or blouse. Have a standard piece of attire, which includes black shoes and socks (appropriate stocking for ladies). This one outfit can be used for weddings, communion services, funerals, banquets and semi-formal dinners. If you are extremely visible as a church leader, it may also be wise to include navy blue, white, and off-white outfits. Church leaders should, in my opinion, be very conservative in their dress. Professional dress during service times and church functions, not flashy and bright clothing is always acceptable. Every style sold in the store is not appropriate for ministers and church leaders or even members to wear. Many of the fashions are not made with the builds of African-American men and women in mind. They are European or Italian cut, not African cut. When we wear these clothes, we look stuffed and uncomfortable. It is always a great compliment to me when, even dressed casually, a person may ask, "Are you a minister?" One should carry one's self in a manner and dress representative of Christ and His Church. The minister does need to be tastefully dressed, yet know he is not advertising clothing but rather Christ.

Several years ago, I was doing some shopping at an outlet mall. While I was looking in the men's section, I came upon a noted pastor in our city. We exchanged greetings and discovered that we were limited in our selections due to our sizes. There was one black suit that would fit this pastor. I lifted it to him for him and his wife to inspect. He shared that he did not own a black suit. Each time I have seen this pastor over the last ten years, he has always thanked me for that advice. He has shared that he wore that black suit to many, many functions, and he has always received high compliments.

Every minister needs a black suit. Green and red lizard shoes with a purple suit may have their place, but I would not want a minister wearing psychedelic and loud colors standing over the remains of my loved one or performing the wedding for my daughter. More importantly, the carriers of the Word, the presenters of the gospel, should take great concern in the clothes they wear as they serve the people of God. I know someone will disagree and take issue with this point, yet whether we like it or not, it is distasteful and unprofessional to dress inappropriately for an occasion. Always be dignified in your dress. Wear the best clothes your budget can afford. Even buy the latest style. But there is no need to make a public display or to be noted for what's on your back rather than what's in your head and heart.

Allow me to say one final word. Some church members enjoy wearing jewelry. This is alright if and when it is done in good taste. Some now wear three earrings, four chains around their necks, a ring on every finger and, when they smile, they have so much gold shining on their teeth that it looks like Christmas decorations. However, when in an official capacity, decorative eyeglasses, large bracelets, and noticeable jewelry should be worn minimally. The use of clergy and choir robes originally was designed to cover the person and the position held in life. (Do not pin flowers, corsages or boutonnieres on robes.) But now, we decorate the robes with all kinds of symbols to display our achievements and recognition. Choir members, ushers, nurses, officers, and ministers should wear little, if any, jewelry while serving the church. When and if it is worn, it should be done in uniform only and not with one individual standing out and drawing attention to himself. The purpose of the church is to lift up Christ and not flesh. Tight pants and blue jeans for women should be avoided. Some churches feel that women should not wear pants at all, especially in the church. I feel that if the pants men and women wear are two sizes too small, they are inappropriate for public and church functions. Many of our churches now have female ministers. These ministers should always remember that they are not only called ministers in the pulpit on Sunday morning. They must always dress modestly. In the pulpit, they should wear at least knee length dresses or skirts. If the outfit is long enough, then there is no need to place fancy lace handkerchiefs, which just happen to match the outfit, over her knees. When men and women sit in the pulpit, all eyes are focused on them and all should be properly covered. Once I saw a sister who wore a very short dress. All during the service she was pulling on it to cover herself. I wanted to say to the lady, "Stop pulling on your dress, because you don't have any more to pull."

# SUCCESSFUL DRESSING

Guidelines for both Men and Women, written by The Fulton County Extension Service, AWW/ CHL/1983

## *Men*

A two or three-piece suit idea is always appropriate. A nice shirt and tie makes this a smart outfit.

Do have your ankles covered. Wear socks that are mid-calf length at least. Socks should stay up; those with worn elastic should be tossed or fixed.

Do wear a tie. Do not have your collar lying open.

Keep shirts tucked inside your pants.

Shave as often as needed. A 5 o'clock shadow at 9 a.m. is out.

Check out the dress codes. Jeans are not proper to wear everywhere. If jeans are permitted, be sure they're neat, clean, mended, and not too broken in.

Jogging pants are too casual. A dressier pair of pants looks better.

Trade in your worn sneakers for a great pair of loafers or string-up oxfords.

## *Women*

Wear medium heeled shoes that have a closed toe or narrow opening at the toe.

Wear an under-slip that is the right length and does not show. A slip that's too long looks plain sloppy and a blouse you can see through without a slip or camisole underneath is worse.

Wear just one bangle bracelet, too many will clang.

Easy on any jewelry, a few pieces of jewelry play up an outfit. Too much can detract. When in doubt, remove one piece.

Hose should be a natural color, maybe a shade darker than your skin tone. No bright colors and no snags or runs.

Ladies, makeup can make you look terrific – if you wear it the right way! Not too much! It should look natural and well blended.

The outfit should make you look serious. If you're looking for attention you'll get it in a low-cut dress. Save the party outfit for after hours. Avoid extremes.

Pants shouldn't be too tight, and not too baggy.

Find the right skirt length for you. You don't have to change with the tides. Just below the knee is good for most ladies and most activities.

# Summary of 12 Points

Point One – Be on time.

Point Two – Never pass up the aisle during prayer or scripture reading.

Point Three – Be respectful of the worship service.

Point Four – Be devout in every attitude.

Point Five – Be thoughtful of the comfort of others.

Point Six – Speak a bright cheery word to as many as possible.

Point Seven – Proper address the pulpit and church body.

Point Eight – Never put on your coat or wrap during the closing hymn.

Point Nine – There should be no loud talking or jesting after the service is concluded.

Point Ten – Let reverence be the keyword.

Point Eleven – During prayer, all heads should be bowed and all eyes closed.

Point Twelve – Always dress modestly as becomes Christians.

# We Speak Life

**We set forth this great work ...
we claim glory not gloom;
riches not rubble;
peace not problems;
and fellowship not fear.**

Enjoy the dynamic motivational preaching and inspirational speaking of Dr. William E. Flippin, Sr., Sylvia T. Flippin and their three sons, Reverend William E. Flippin, Jr., Reverend Richard C. Flippin and Reverend Joseph C. T. Flippin. They are available for church services, special programs, revivals, seminars and lecturers. These great preachers and speakers have traveled throughout this nation delivering enthusiastic speeches and soul stirring sermons to churches, colleges and conventions.